CAREER PLANNING

Created Specially for Tech Academy Graduates Who Are Working in Tech

Erik D. Gross and Jack C. Stanley,
Co-Founders of The Tech Academy

WHEN TO USE THIS GUIDE

This Career Planning Guide is for Tech Academy graduates who are working in tech.

It serves to answer the question, "You are on the job; now what?"

If you are not yet working in tech, hold off on using this Guide and instead work with our Job Placement team to secure a technology position.

Otherwise, read on!

INTRODUCTION

Congratulations! You have landed your first job post-graduation. We are sure you are equal parts excited and nervous.

We wrote this Guide to give you expert guidance on how to strategically navigate the first three years of your tech career.

Even if you have already been working in the technology sector for a while, we encourage you to work through each of the phases detailed herein.

Taken from our own experience in tech, and in helping thousands of graduates to succeed long term in the technology sector, this Guide is full of practical, sequenced advice and resources to help you cement and add to your knowledge, decide on and solidify the broad directions of your tech career, and continually add to the soft skills so vital to on-the-job success and career advancement.

We are very proud of you for completing your boot camp training, and hope this Guide serves you well as you embark on your journey as a technology professional.

Erik D. Gross and Jack C. Stanley,
Co-Founders of The Tech Academy

HOW TO USE THIS GUIDE

This Guide exists for two reasons:

Reason #1: So that you will be an active member of The Tech Academy Accelerator (an affordable monthly subscription service that includes weekly workshops with Erik Gross), and also avail yourself of our advanced training services, so we can help you implement everything you read here.

Reason #2: To give you a comprehensive approach to self-directed career progress that is immediately valuable, so that you will actually want to do Reason #1 as quickly as possible.

As you have likely come to see as you worked through your boot camp, graduated, and successfully got hired, WE REALLY CARE ABOUT YOU AND YOUR SUCCESS IN THE TECH INDUSTRY.

We want to help you at every step of your career.

To that end, we have structured this Guide for the first 36 months of your career in tech as follows (as we mentioned earlier, these tips also apply to those who have already been working in tech for months or years):

1. First, we will cover what to work on during the **first 6 months** in the industry. During this time period, you will want to cement what you learned in your boot camp, build up your network of peers and mentors, and dive deep in a few tech skills and tools that can quickly differentiate you at your job.

2. Next, we will lay out a plan for the next year – from **months 6-18**. This is where you will make important decisions about whether to specialize or become a generalist, start to actively shape your public presence as a technology professional, deepen your technical skills in vital areas (like the cloud), and focus on the soft skills that are actually your biggest levers for achieving long-term success in the field.

3. Finally, we will talk about how to navigate the next 18 months (**months 18-36**), getting you to the three year mark from graduation. By this time, your self-confidence should be much greater, so it will be time to concentrate on advancement and leadership. We will give you expert guidance on developing into a leader without offending your peers, improving your

public speaking and presentation skills, and becoming skilled at negotiation and conflict resolution. In addition, we will talk about how to increase your compensation, without burning bridges.

To summarize:

- FIRST 6 MONTHS: solidify bootcamp knowledge, build personal network, and learn new tech skills.

- 6 MONTHS IN - 1.5 YEAR MARK: decide upon specialist or generalist, shape public presence, deepen technical skills, and enhance soft skills.

- 1.5 YEARS IN - 3 YEAR MARK: focus on career advancement, develop leadership, improve public speaking, hone negotiation skills, and increase compensation.

In each section, we will give you the VITAL ACTIONS (tasks we consider mandatory) to concentrate on during that time period, followed by the OPTIONAL ACTIONS (tasks which are recommended, yet not required) which you should concentrate on as you make time available.

Again, you may be reading this after you have started your career. It should still be very valuable to you. There are likely some recommendations here which you have not yet implemented, or which can be improved upon.

We sincerely believe that knowledge workers are among the most valuable people in society, and that a skilled, well-rounded technology professional can make incredible contributions in business and (if this is important to you) in social and humanitarian areas as well. All while being very well compensated and living a balanced, rewarding life.

This Guide has been created to help make that vision a reality for you.

FOREVER TASKS

In later portions of this Guide, you will study breakdowns of what to focus on at various time periods in the beginning years of your tech career. For example, there are certain actions to take in the beginning months, which are less important a couple years in.

Yet, there are also actions that *always* apply from here on out. So, let's first cover the minimum points that you should focus on at all times as a Tech Academy graduate, from this moment on.

HERE ARE THE VITAL CONTINUING ACTIONS TO APPLY FOREVER AS A GRADUATE OF THE TECH ACADEMY:

1. BE AN ACTIVE MEMBER OF THE TECH ACADEMY COMMUNITY.

2. ALWAYS BE LEARNING.

Let's take a deeper look into these two points.

BE AN ACTIVE MEMBER OF THE TECH ACADEMY COMMUNITY

Stay connected with the school and be involved in our alumni network. Here are some specifics on how to participate in Tech Academy activities:

1. Join The Tech Academy Alumni Meetup Events group (meetup.com/TTA-Alumni-Meetup) and attend our alumni meetup events.

2. Read our Monthly Alumni Newsletters, Daily Student Emails, and other updates that we email out.

3. Attend other Tech Academy events (meetup.com/techacademy/events).

4. Be a speaker at one of our weekly Tech Talks (you can arrange this by contacting our Job Placement staff).

There are other ways to be active, such as sending in referrals, or simply answering communication you receive from us.

The Tech Academy's mission statement is: TO GRADUATE ENTRY-LEVEL TECHNOLOGY PROFESSIONALS THAT EXCEL IN THE BASICS OF THEIR FIELD AND THEREAFTER HAVE SUCCESSFUL CAREERS IN THE TECH INDUSTRY, AND WHOSE ACTIONS RAISE INDUSTRY STANDARDS AND SURPASS CLIENT EXPECTATIONS.

That mission does not end when you land your first tech job! You are forever and always a part of The Tech Academy family, so the first recommendation we have for you is to keep that connection alive.

ALWAYS BE LEARNING

In the rapidly evolving tech industry, it is vital to never cease expanding your skills and knowledge. This is necessary in order to stay current with new technologies and methodologies, ensuring relevance and competitiveness in one's career. To that end, here is how to "always be learning" as a Tech Academy graduate:

1. Attend the weekly Tech Academy Accelerator workshops, and complete the relevant classes and watch the applicable videos included in your subscription library. We grant students and graduates access for an extensive free trial period, followed by a nominal monthly fee. It is grossly underpriced, and exponentially worth it! Here's our graduate-only registration link:

    bit.ly/ttagraduate

2. Enroll in our specialty training classes (we offer these at a 50% discount for graduates). These courses cover a wide array of additional, more advanced technology specialties that were not covered on your boot camp, and include such subjects as: artificial

intelligence, design, video game development, data science, cybersecurity, and many, many more.

Each of these are valuable skill sets that can easily be tacked onto your knowledge base, thereby increasing your employability and promotability. To obtain descriptions, pricing, and more info about The Tech Academy's advanced training courses (such as our brand-new Artificial Intelligence Developer Course), contact our Admissions Office:

email: **info@learncodinganywhere.com**   phone: **(503)206-6915**

We also recommend that you subscribe to Pluralsight and give yourself the goal of completing one course on that platform each month.

Yes, implementing these points can cost money. But just like your boot camp, such training is an investment in yourself – and *you are worth it*. In order to move up in tech, you must increase your skills and experience, and the above actions help you accomplish that.

As an aside, your employer may have programs to reimburse you for some of your continuing education as a tech professional.

With the orientation to your "forever tasks" in place, let's now lay out the plan for your first three years in tech!

PHASE 1: YOUR FIRST SIX MONTHS

As we covered earlier in this Guide, each phase of your first three years of working in tech is broken into two types of recommendations:

1. **Vital actions:** These are the minimum tasks you should focus on no matter what. If you are serious about "climbing the tech ladder" and increasing your compensation, these are the absolute necessities.

2. **Optional actions:** These are the nice-to-have items that you can work on if you choose, *after* you have the vital actions under control. Consider these strongly recommended, but not absolutely required.

IF YOU COMPLETE ALL VITAL AND OPTIONAL ACTIONS, YOUR LONG-TERM SUCCESS IN THE TECH INDUSTRY IS ABSOLUTELY ASSURED.

VITAL ACTIONS

During day one through month six in the tech industry, here are the areas you should concentrate on:

- CONSOLIDATE AND STRENGTHEN YOUR BOOT CAMP EDUCATION.

- BUILD YOUR NETWORK OF PEERS AND MENTORS.

- GAIN DEEP EXPERTISE IN A SMALL NUMBER OF VITAL DIFFERENTIATING SKILLS.

Let's break each of these down, one at a time.

Vital action: Consolidating and Strengthening your Boot Camp Education

There is a lot to learn on any one of our boot camps. Yet, chances are, for even the most successful Tech Academy student, there are certain subjects or skills that you feel like you could be better at.

For sure, as we covered earlier, a major part of a tech career is continuous learning. The best place to start in the beginning of your career is *not* necessarily adding in a whole lot of new knowledge. Believe us, you will already have enough new subjects to learn simply due to the needs of your new job. There, you will use your self-training skills gained at our school to quickly get up to speed on what's needed to succeed in your first tasks on the job.

And so, for this step, what we're talking about is taking dedicated time to scan through your boot camp courses and identify areas you know you should shore up.

The MOST IMPORTANT exercise you can take here is this: ONCE YOU HAVE FOUND ONE OR MORE SUBJECTS YOU KNOW YOU WANT TO CONCENTRATE ON, GO THROUGH THEM AND LOOK FOR ANY WORDS OR SYMBOLS YOU ARE NOT 100% CONFIDENT OF IN YOUR UNDERSTANDING.

This is *vitally* important. Your inability to understand and apply any subject you are trying to master has, at its root, misunderstood terms or symbols. ALWAYS DEFINE WORDS YOU DO NOT UNDERSTAND. It starts here, with this Guide. If we use a term you don't know the meaning of, research the definition online.

This should be your highest priority when reviewing your boot camp materials – and frankly, in all of your studies.

Having done that, you should concentrate on actually *using* those skills by building things. Besides the fact that you will likely be using many of these skills on the job, you should also consider doing some projects that make use of these skills you're restudying.

Some suggestions on how to make the most of this process:

1. Store everything you do here out on your GitHub account.

2. Optional: do projects with one or two other people who want to practice the same skills.

3. USE VERSION CONTROL ON ALL PROJECTS – even if you are going at it alone.

4. If you do work with others on a project, address your Git workflow. Agree on a pattern to follow, document it in your README file, and follow it – again, whether it is just you, a small team, or large group.

5. For extra value, find a way to publish aspects of this work online. This could be as simple as recording your working sessions and posting them on Twitch or YouTube.

So, to summarize this first point:

1. REVIEW THE CONTENT YOU STUDIED ON YOUR BOOT CAMP.

2. APPLY THE DATA COVERED ON YOUR BOOT CAMP.

Vital action: Building your network of peers and mentors

You will for sure be developing a network of peers and mentors at your new job. However, it's important here to start growing your network in the wider technology industry.

There are two main divisions of activity here: online and in-person.

Your online work here should be driven by your personal interests. We recommend looking for, and following, any online source of data or opinion about the aspects of technology that are most interesting to you. Don't forget to consider the soft skills aspect of tech here.

You may find there are certain voices that you really enjoy learning from. Start to engage with their community. Be polite and interested. Ask questions. Respond to questions if you feel you have got something of value to say.

At a certain point, you may want to connect directly to people you'd like to have in your network. LinkedIn is great for this, of course – but you will find lots of ways to connect. Again, be kind and interested and you will have great success. One of the most valuable things you can do here is to find some helpful way to contribute, in a way that advances the goals of the person or group.

Offline, you should use some of your time to find interest groups in your area. The same approach you use for online interaction works here – you may gradually find a few groups, or people, that you have affinity and admiration for. Start to get involved – attend meetups to see if there's some way you can help.

Finally, let's look at the subject of mentors. If your company has a formal mentorship program, sign up. If not, ask around and see if there's an informal mentorship culture there. If those aren't fruitful, look to your online or in-person network.

More specifically, to find a suitable mentor outside of your company: actively participate in online forums, social media groups, and platforms like LinkedIn, focusing on areas of technology that interest you, and engage with content from potential mentors by asking insightful questions and sharing valuable insights.

Additionally, attend industry meetups, conferences, and workshops in your area, where you can meet professionals with experience and expertise in your field of interest, and initiate conversations that could lead to mentorship opportunities. When you meet someone more skilled than you, who you admire and respect, you can ask them to mentor you.

A word on being a mentee: have an idea put together of what outcome you're looking for, be respectful of your mentor's time, and approach the relationship with a willingness to learn and to move out of your comfort zone.

Let's summarize this point:

1. GROW YOUR NETWORK BEYOND THE WORKPLACE, including:

    A. ONLINE NETWORKING, and

    B. IN-PERSON NETWORKING.

2. FIND A MENTOR AND LEARN FROM THEM.

Vital action: Gaining deep expertise in differentiating skills

There are a few technical and soft skills you can work on in this first stage of your career that can set the stage for future success. Here's what we recommend:

1. VERSION CONTROL. Every engineering team needs a Subject Matter Expert (SME) on version control. Sure, you know the basics – and 90% of the time, those basic skills will be sufficient. But it is pretty much a sure thing that at some point, a repo will get FUBAR (look it up if you don't know the term; we're not going to swear here). Gnarly version control

issues can stop dev work cold – and being the person who can dive in and sort it all out is a very valuable skill that can set you apart in your career.

2. THE CLOUD. There is no getting away from it. In fact, we call this out in later phases of your first three years. But getting started early with the cloud will be a big factor in making you more and more valuable over time. Believe it or not, there are many technologists who are not that cloud literate – and cloud competency is rapidly becoming a requirement.

3. COLLABORATING WITH NON-TECHNICAL FOLKS. As a Tech Academy graduate, you have a secret weapon – the training program you went through has armed you with the ability to explain complex technical concepts in a clear manner, for any audience. This is rare in the tech industry, and is *very* appreciated by your non-technical colleagues. Work on this; it will be a key part of your success over time.

OPTIONAL ACTIONS

If you are successfully applying the vital actions we just covered and make more time available, this is what we advise during this period to accelerate your career:

- LEARN A NEW PROGRAMMING LANGUAGE.

- TURN YOUR PORTFOLIO INTO A THING OF BEAUTY.

- "BUILD IN PUBLIC" WITH A PEER.

Optional action: Learning a new programming language

This is an important step in becoming a well-rounded tech professional.

There are so many to choose from: Java, C#, C, C++, PHP, Swift, R, Objective-C, and more!

With the knowledge base you gained on your boot camp, you will find the process of adding an additional language to your tool belt a relatively easy activity. While there will be moments of frustration and difficulty, these languages all utilize the five elements of a computer program, and share similarities with other high-level languages.

Often, you will already have a desire to learn a specific language. If so, that should be your first choice. There is no substitute for personal interest in terms of driving effective self-learning.

The next area to look at is languages that are in use at your company but aren't used in your main work.

Finally, you can survey to see what languages you don't already know are popular – Stack Overflow does an annual developer survey that can help here.

Here is a basic approach to learning a new programming language that we've found helpful over the years:

1. LEARN HOW TO IMPLEMENT THE "FIVE ELEMENTS OF A COMPUTER PROGRAM" IN THE NEW LANGUAGE. You can find these in Overview of Software Development Course in your boot camp materials; we also have a great article on the subject in each of our *Learn Coding Basics in Hours* books. No need to make an application of any magnitude here; just work out how the new language approaches building these five elements.

2. DO A TUTORIAL IN THE NEW LANGUAGE. A couple of important notes on this step:

    a. First, pick a tutorial that attempts to teach ONLY the new language, not "language plus a bunch of extra things that the author is super excited about."

    b. Second, do the tutorial exactly as it is laid out – don't try to create an application of your own in the language yet.

3. BUILD A PROJECT OF YOUR OWN CREATION WITH THE LANGUAGE. This is a great point at which to involve one or more friends or coworkers, as described in the "Build in Public" section below.

Optional action: Turning your portfolio into a thing of beauty

For many people in the tech industry, your GitHub profile will be one of the first things they look at when they first find out about you. It should represent you well.

A simple Google search or ChatGPT conversation can give you some great ideas on what to do here, so we're not going to write out a full plan for this step.

That said, we have some advice:

1. Don't take a ton of time to do this. There is a point of diminishing returns here; just make it good.

2. If you maintain one or more other portfolio sites (which is common; perhaps you have hosted some of the apps you have created, or you have a portfolio of your design work), make sure you feature links to those in your GitHub profile.

Optional action: "Building in Public" with a peer

Like it or not, your online presence will be highly influential in your career. The time to start "making a name for yourself" is not when you're in the middle of your next job search. Instead, you should start to build up, over time, a record of what you do as a technologist.

A very effective way to do this is to take the work you're already doing to learn and practice tech skills and make that learning process public.

There are many ways to do this, and there is no one perfect platform for it. The basic principles, though, can apply to any online medium or platform:

1. FIND A FEW PEOPLE TO PARTNER WITH WHO ARE INTERESTED IN THE TECH SKILL YOU'RE CONCENTRATING ON. They don't necessarily need to be at your current point in your career; often, you will find an experienced tech professional who wants to learn the same thing. Regardless, what you're looking for is people who are curious, kind, and helpful – and who won't mind having the learning process presented to the world online.

2. DOCUMENT THE WHOLE PROCESS – MISTAKES AND ALL. Any technologist worth their salt knows that the learning process involves lots of trial and error. In fact, the people who end up following along with your learning journey will appreciate a realistic, unvarnished look at what it takes to learn a new subject and apply it to making a real piece of software.

Once you hit the six month mark in your tech career, we move onto Phase 2, which you will focus on for the next year.

PHASE 2: YOUR FIRST 18 MONTHS

Phase 2 covers months 6-18 of working in tech. You will most likely still be working in the same job at this point, but you are no longer the "new guy" or "new girl."

VITAL ACTIONS

After six months of working in the tech industry, here are the areas you should concentrate on over the following year:

- DECIDE ON A BROAD CAREER STRATEGY: SPECIALIST OR GENERALIST?

- BUILD UP YOUR SOFT SKILLS.

- GO DEEP ON YOUR CLOUD KNOWLEDGE.

- GET THE CLOUD FUNDAMENTALS CERTIFICATION WITH YOUR CLOUD SERVICE PROVIDER OF CHOICE.

Now, let's take up each one of these points.

Vital action: Deciding on Specialist or Generalist?

This is a particularly important decision. First, let us describe what we mean by a *specialist* and a *generalist*.

SPECIALIST: A specialist will devote themselves to developing deep expertise in a specific technology, or related family of technologies. There is some nuance here; this can also mean primarily working in one specific industry, or in related industries.

The basic principle is that you would choose a technology or an industry, preferably one that looks like it will be around for the long term, and work very hard to know that technology or industry inside and out.

Examples might include:
- The Microsoft Dynamics suite of products

- Database development
- Blockchain development
- The finance industry

PROS OF BEING A SPECIALIST: As a SME in the area, you will often qualify for high-paying roles where a deep level of experience and expertise is required – you can solve difficult problems which someone with less skill might take a long time to solve. In addition, you may find ways to monetize this deep knowledge in various ways as you gain experience – through information-based businesses such as author, course creator or consultant.

CONS OF BEING A SPECIALIST: Your job search process may become more challenging, as the high-paying roles you are interested in may be less common. You also risk being affected by major changes in the market that make your skill set less valuable – or altogether worthless. In that case, you will have a challenge to reinvent yourself as an expert in another discipline.

GENERALIST: A generalist, on the other hand, will endeavor to become knowledgeable and skilled in a wide variety of technologies and industries. Essentially, they are continually adding to the *range* of their knowledge and skill. This is not to say they don't have deep expertise in any area – far from it. The difference is that they are not trying to concentrate primarily on roles in their preferred technology or industry.

PROS OF BEING A GENERALIST: As you gain extensive experience in a wide variety of technologies and industries, you will find yourself gaining strong insight into the abstract concepts behind how technology is applied in many different scenarios – and you will consequently be gaining a deeper understanding of the fundamental principles underlying the most important aspects of technology, software development and business operations.

This path can lead you to succeed in tech and people leadership, systems architecture, and cross-functional collaboration. Finally, you may find yourself gaining increased confidence in confronting and solving "wicked problems" – problems that contain a great degree of ambiguity, and for which a clear path to resolution is not immediately visible.

CONS OF BEING A GENERALIST: In the initial parts of your career, you may find that standing out among your peers is more challenging, as you might not be known as the "[blank] expert". In addition, you may move a bit more often from role to role, or from employer to employer, as you seek to purposely increase your range of experience.

In addition, this approach requires you to concentrate your personal learning on subjects not commonly found in company training initiatives (because they don't immediately result in skills needed for specific technology initiatives at the company). These are covered in some detail later in this guide, and include:

- The philosophy of "First Principles": A problem-solving approach that involves breaking down complex problems into their most basic, fundamental elements.

- Principles and strategies for idea generation and innovation: Techniques and methodologies for coming up with new ideas and creative solutions.

- The discipline known as "Design Thinking": A user-centered approach to problem-solving that encourages empathy, collaboration, and iterative testing of concepts and prototypes.

In terms of deciding between the specialist and the generalist paths, there is no right or wrong answer here – either will lead you to long-term career success if you apply all you learned in your boot camp. And again, these two approaches are not mutually exclusive, and have significant overlap.

You may be wondering: "Why am I deciding on whether to be a specialist or generalist now, and not earlier in my career – or even before I land my first tech job?"

There are two answers to this question:

1. When one is first entering the tech industry, they can't afford to be too picky about their job/position. Getting one's foot in the door is the hardest part, and future jobs are much easier to secure.

2. Frankly, you did not yet have enough experience to make an informed decision.

Finally, don't stress about this decision – you will hopefully have a long and rewarding career in tech, and you will have plenty of opportunities to reinvent yourself.

Vital action: Building up your soft skills

By this time, you should be feeling a bit more confident in your ability to contribute as part of a team, and some of the "imposter syndrome" should be getting better.

Now is a perfect time to concentrate on building up the soft skills that are so necessary for long-term success in the tech industry. Specifically, you should study and practice these skills:

- TEAMWORK AND COLLABORATION: Focus on developing strong teamwork skills, understanding different team dynamics, and working effectively in diverse groups.

- PROBLEM-SOLVING: Enhance your ability to work with others to troubleshoot and solve problems creatively, a highly-valued skill in any tech role.

- FEEDBACK RECEPTION AND ADAPTATION: Learn to receive feedback constructively and use it to improve your work and professional relationships.

A massive step in the right direction on this step is: GET AND READ OUR BOOK: *The Small Talk Secret: How to Overcome Introversion and Anxiety So You Can Talk to Anyone*.

You can get a copy for free here (just pay shipping and handling): bit.ly/freesmalltalk

Vital action: Going deep on your cloud knowledge

We have already called this out as an important area. At this stage of your early career, though, it is time to really double down on the cloud.

The strategy here is simple:

1. If you don't yet have foundational knowledge in the cloud, start there. Pick your cloud provider of choice (Azure, Amazon Web Services or Google Cloud Platform), and study the material they test for on their foundational certification.

2. If you already have strong knowledge in cloud fundamentals, begin to study how the cloud applies to your main area of expertise – that is, if you're a developer, study cloud development; if you're primarily a Data Science professional, study cloud services in that area; etc.

THE IMPORTANT THING HERE IS TO PUT CLOUD SKILLS AT THE TOP OF YOUR PERSONAL LEARNING STRATEGY.

Vital action: Getting a cloud fundamentals certification

In general, certifications don't hold much water in the tech industry. Engineers and technologists usually care a lot more about your technical skills, willingness to learn, and ability to collaborate in solving difficult problems than they do the paper you can hang on the wall.

Cloud certifications are changing all that. A cloud certificate tells others two vital things:

1. You know how to apply your skills in an on-premises environment, and

2. You have taken the time to gain an understanding of how to do those same things in a new, cloud-centric way.

They are seen by both peers and leaders as the sign of a professional.

The task here is simple: Study for, and pass, the fundamental cloud certification for your preferred cloud provider.

Here is how to go about obtaining cloud certification with each of the top providers:

GOOGLE CLOUD: CERTIFIED DIGITAL LEADER

1. Complete this learning path in full:

    cloudskillsboost.google/paths/9

2. Register for and take the exam here:

    cloud.google.com/learn/certification/cloud-digital-leader

AMAZON WEB SERVICES: CLOUD PRACTITIONER

   Prepare for, register for and complete the exam here:

   aws.amazon.com/certification/certified-cloud-practitioner

MICROSOFT AZURE: MICROSOFT AZURE FUNDAMENTALS (AZ-900)

Prepare for, register for and complete the exam here:

bit.ly/azurecertificationprep

OPTIONAL ACTIONS

- CREATE AND EXECUTE A STRATEGY FOR PUBLIC VISIBILITY.

- BEGIN CONTRIBUTING TO OPEN-SOURCE PROJECTS.

- FILL IN COMPUTER SCIENCE TRAINING NOT COVERED IN YOUR BOOT CAMP.

Optional action: Creating a strategy for public visibility

As covered briefly earlier, your public persona will be a vital aspect of your tech career. This includes both your online presence, and your in-person network and reputation.

It is to your advantage to start working on this aspect early in your career. For one thing, it can take some time to develop your unique "voice" in terms of how you communicate to the world. For another, one of the most important aspects of public persona, regardless of how you choose to present yourself, is *time*. To a great extent, you are as real to others as you are present online. Having an extensive record of your professional and personal activities, over a long period of time, makes you more real and will eventually pay off in countless ways.

While an entire book could be written on this subject, and we in fact address aspects of this part of your career often in our Tech Academy Accelerator and our various career coaching and training services, here we will lay out a foundational plan to get started in this area.

The first decision to be made here in terms of a public presence is to decide on a medium you will use to publish online. For the most part, this really comes down to personal preference. Some general guidelines here:

- If you are more comfortable writing, you should look at blogs, newsletters or long-form social media posts.

- If you prefer speaking, but don't necessarily want to be on camera, you should consider podcasts.

- And if you are comfortable on camera, you can look at YouTube or Twitch channels, or video podcasts.

PRO TIP: Most of these approaches result in content that you can repurpose in other forms. For example, if you record a video or audio podcast, you can easily convert the audio to written form and use that text in a blog or in long-form articles.

Regardless of the medium you prefer, you should choose one – and just get started. Often it feels odd at first, and can be a bit overwhelming and even embarrassing – but the truth is that even early in your career, you have valuable knowledge and insights that can help people earlier in their journey than you are. And before long, you will get more comfortable with the process. It is pretty surprising how quickly you can build up an extensive body of your content and knowledge out in the world.

As a final note on your public presence, you should optimize your LinkedIn profile at this point. There is a lot of information online about strategies for this process; the books by John Nemo are particularly good.

Optional action: Contributing to open-source projects

While this is not required for long-term success in tech, it can be one of the most rewarding things you can do in your career. It can also lead to deep friendships and valuable connections, opening doors for you later in your career.

To help you if you're interested in this area, we've included a complete Guide to getting started in open source software contribution as an appendix to this Guide.

Optional action: Filling in Computer Science training

While we cover some of the more vital aspects of formal Computer Science in our boot camps, we are limited by time to only teaching the fundamentals of the subject – those principles you need in order to become a well-rounded, entry-level technology professional.

There is much important data in the subject, though – information that will be essential to you as you rise into more senior technology roles.

Therefore, it is important that you integrate Computer Science subjects into your personal study strategy.

While there are many resources online for this material, most are unnecessarily confusing. In particular, you should avoid any free materials from colleges or universities until AFTER you have solidified your Computer Science knowledge.

A good resource is the book "A Programmer's Guide to Computer Science: A virtual degree for the self-taught developer". You can find it here: a.co/d/460s3Yz

We also cover Computer Science concepts often in our Accelerator and advanced training services.

PHASE 3: GETTING TO THE THREE-YEAR MARK

Phase 3 covers the final 18 months of your first three years working in tech. Let's discuss the minimum areas of concentration for this final time period.

VITAL ACTIONS

Now that you have been working in tech for a year and a half, these are the points to focus on:

- CHART OUT YOUR NEXT THREE CAREER MILESTONES.

- TAKE ON A LEADERSHIP ROLE, NO MATTER HOW LARGE OR SMALL.

- BUILD YOUR PRESENTATION SKILLS AND PRESENT WITHIN YOUR COMPANY.

- NEGOTIATE A SIGNIFICANT INCREASE IN COMPENSATION.

Vital action: Charting out your next three career milestones

Regardless of what your first tech position is, there is most certainly room for growth. However, it is important to guide that growth yourself, instead of leaving it to chance.

By this point in your career, you will have started to identify what you look for in tech roles. This is the time to start planning the next few steps up the career ladder.

The place to start is usually right where you're working. Hopefully your employer has clearly defined career tracks for the various roles in the organization; sometimes they do not. Regardless, you should talk to your leader about your future career track. They should help you articulate your goals, develop a strategy to attain them, and give you guidance on how to prepare for advancement while succeeding in your current role.

This plan does not need to be set in stone; however, any plan is better than no plan. Take the time here to plan your future.

Vital action: Taking on a leadership role

Some people are drawn to leadership and some are not. Regardless of your general temperament on this subject, it is difficult to advance well in tech without putting some attention on your ability to lead others.

For many, this is not a formal job role – it is a natural consequence of their having developed expertise in one or more areas, and of having that expertise noticed by others. Here, your leadership may be more of a casual thing – but developing your confidence in leadership is no less important in this case than if you were given a formal role as a leader. A senior technologist, regardless of their discipline, is expected to guide people and projects.

For others, leadership can be a more official designation.

In either case, you should pay attention to a few things as you work to become effective in any leadership role you find yourself in:

1. You may struggle with feeling like you will lose connection with, and the respect of your peers if you move into a leadership role. A whole book could be written about this (and many have been, actually), but one thing to consider is this: Any enterprise, in order to function well and attain its goals, needs leaders. Often, a reluctant leader can be more effective than one who wants the position for personal reasons. Why not take on the role and apply your sense of professionalism and care to it? You will grow in the process, and also help to assure long-term survival for your team and your company.

2. A good leader pays close attention to what already works in an area, only changing things after careful observation and with the advice of those most familiar with the area.

Talk to your people leader about your thoughts and goals in this area; they usually appreciate your initiative and care for the team, and can give you valuable guidance.

Vital action: Building your presentation skills

Developing the skill of advocating for your ideas and projects is an extremely important factor in long-term success in the tech industry. Whether it is in your team, in front of the whole engineering org, or anywhere in between – those who can effectively communicate ideas stand out from the crowd – and make a huge difference in the workplace.

This is one where you may really need to stretch – many people struggle with public speaking. The best resource we can recommend for gaining and improving your skill and confidence in this area is Toastmasters.

From their website (toastmasters.org): *"Toastmasters International is a nonprofit educational organization that builds confidence and teaches public speaking skills through a worldwide network of clubs that meet online and in person. In a supportive community or corporate environment, members prepare and deliver speeches, respond to impromptu questions, and give and receive constructive feedback. It is through this regular practice that members are empowered to meet personal and professional communication goals."*

Find a local club, sign up and apply yourself industriously to the work. It will help you in every area of your life, but of course in your career advancement.

Vital: Negotiating a significant increase in compensation

Now is the step that most readers probably skipped ahead to: higher pay!

If you have not already gotten a significant raise up to this point, it is time to work on it actively.

While there is a lot of information available about this area, there are a few pieces of important data we want to impart about this often-harrowing process:

1. Never lose sight of your value. You are a trained technology professional, solving difficult problems in a domain that most people are intimidated by and don't understand. In addition, you are a Tech Academy graduate – you think like an engineer; you can break down complex technical subjects for any audience; and you can effectively self-teach. You have great worth.

2. Creating a record of your primary accomplishments on the job can help you prepare for conversations about pay. You should be prepared to explain your value to the organization. One way to do this is to update your resume.

3. Unless you are unhappy with your company as a whole, you should first look to your current employer for this raise. Your accumulated domain knowledge and experience in

how the company operates likely makes you more valuable in your current company than you might be in another company.

4. If you don't succeed in your current company, and you do look for and secure a new job elsewhere, do NOT try to pit the new employer against your current employer in a "bidding war". This can backfire in many ways. Make your decision on your own, deciding what is the best decision for your long-term goals.

Simply put: if you are unhappy where you are, and do not see room for growth, it is now time to apply the data on our Job Placement Course, and to land a higher-paying job that is a better fit.

OPTIONAL ACTIONS

- GET BOOKED AS A SPEAKER AT A TECH CONFERENCE.

- BEGIN MENTORING JUNIOR TECHNOLOGY PROFESSIONALS.

- FOCUS ON DEVELOPING SKILLS FOR INNOVATION AND HANDLING AMBIGUOUS PROBLEMS.

Optional action: Getting booked as a speaker

Besides writing a book, there are few things as beneficial to your public persona as delivering public talks in the industry. While this one is not for everyone, it can help you a lot in the long term.

There are many opportunities for such speaking engagements. You should begin by looking up conferences that address your areas of interest. The web sites for most of these will have a section covering how to apply to be a speaker. There are also websites that aggregate information from many different conferences, so you can search for opportunities more easily. What you are looking for is open "Calls For Proposals", or CFPs – this is how the event organizer lets the community know what topics they would like to have spoken about at the event.

Also, as we mentioned in the "forever actions" section of this Guide, you can always be the speaker at one of The Tech Academy's weekly Tech Talks.

A few simple tips for putting together an effective presentation:

1. Try to get examples of successful presentations from the event organizer, if possible.

2. When making slides for your talk, LESS IS MORE. Do not put a ton of information on your slides – instead, put just enough that you will be reminded of what you want to say.

3. Consider delivering the talk ahead of time to your peers to get practice (and to get over your nervousness).

Optional action: Beginning to mentor junior-level workers

Before you have a decent amount of experience in tech under your belt, the idea of mentoring anyone may seem unreal to you. By the time you have been working in tech for a couple of years, however, you will be shocked by how much you have learned – much of it from generous co-workers, friends and mentors. It may be time to "pay it forward".

Some tips for getting started:

- If your employer has a formal mentoring program, look into how it works and apply to be a mentor.

- If you're already working with a mentor, talk to them about how they started in that role.

- Simply offering to help with getting new members of your team up to speed can be a great way to start.

- Never lose sight of what it was like to be new to technology – help others with grace and understanding.

Optional action: Focusing on skills for innovation and handling ambiguous problems

As you gain experience and the confidence of your peers and leaders, you will start to be brought onto projects that are more challenging. One of the more challenging types of problems to solve are those termed "wicked problems."

From IDEO, leaders in the discipline called Design Thinking: wicked problems are "problems that are complex, open-ended, and ambiguous. These are problems that do not lend themselves to easy judgments of 'right' or 'wrong'."

There are three subjects you should study to become very good at handling difficult problems, generating innovation, and creating ideas on demand:

- Design Thinking. Start with the IDEO organization mentioned above: ideo.com

- The philosophy of "First Principles". There are many good books on the subject, and ChatGPT is remarkably good at explaining the subject and how it can be applied in the tech industry.

- The book "A Technique for Producing Ideas" by James Webb Young. This short book is one of the most powerful books you will ever read in terms of how to produce innovative ideas and solutions to problems. You can find it on Amazon: a.co/d/cbhApGL

Finally, every engineer should read the book "Code Simplicity: The Fundamentals of Software" by Max Kanat-Alexander. You can also find it on Amazon: a.co/d/188SeYX

CONCLUSION

There you have it, your Guide to navigating your first three years in the tech industry. We hope this has been of value.

You should revisit this Guide every few months to make sure you're putting each element in place, as it applies to your unique situation.

WE RECOMMEND SETTING UP CALENDAR REMINDERS FOR THE ACTION ITEMS WE INCLUDED IN THIS GUIDE, so that you are regularly notified and don't forget to complete tasks.

Finally, we want to reiterate the value of **staying connected to your Tech Academy community.**

Of course you have our alumni group and our social media channels – but the best thing you can be doing for your long-term career advancement is joining us inside the Tech Academy Accelerator, and availing yourself of our advanced training and career coaching services.

Thank you for reading The Tech Academy's Career Planning Guide, and good luck!

Erik D. Gross and Jack C. Stanley,
Co-Founders of The Tech Academy

APPENDIX: HOW TO CONTRIBUTE TO OPEN SOURCE SOFTWARE (AND WHY)

INTRODUCTION

Getting involved in the open source community (especially early in your career) is a smart move, for many reasons. When you help others, you almost always get help in return. You also make connections that can last your entire career, helping you down the road in ways you won't anticipate.

In this article, we'll cover why you should consider contributing to open source, and how to get started.

WHY SHOULD I GET INVOLVED IN OPEN SOURCE?

Designing, building, deploying and maintaining software is a social activity. This extends to our tech careers – being part of a network of bright, empathetic professionals brings job satisfaction and career opportunities.

Nowhere in tech is this more apparent than in the world of Free and Open Source Software (FOSS) – in FOSS, we build in public, so our contributions are highly visible and are done together with like-minded developers who enjoy helping others.

Finally, by helping to maintain the supply of well-maintained open source software, you're making the benefits of technology accessible around the world.

HOW DO I FIND A PROJECT TO CONTRIBUTE TO?

The good news is that the collaborative, helpful culture of FOSS means maintainers are often receptive to unsolicited offers of help.

Offering your help

Often, you can simply reach out to a maintainer, offering to contribute. Check the web site for your favorite open source project, or their repo.

An example:

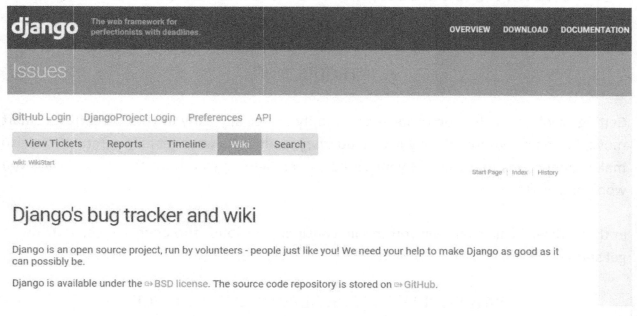

Finding known issues

Most projects keep a list of known issues – often you can find a task that fits your knowledge and experience level.

An example:

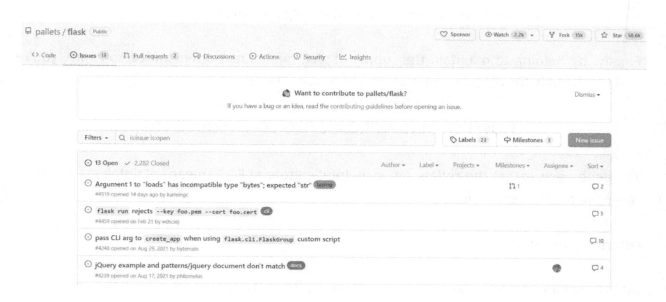

Finding tasks for new contributors

Finally, many maintainers take the time to mark specific issues as being better for new contributors.

An example:

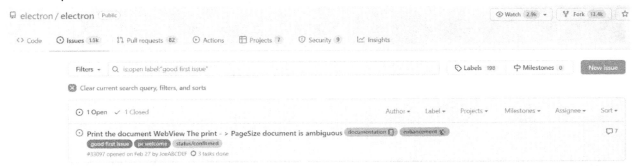

Notice the "Labels" selector to the right – you can use this to filter, showing you the best issues to start with.

OKAY, I HAVE AN ISSUE TO WORK ON – HOW DO I GET STARTED?

The basic process is the same for nearly all projects – but be sure to read the contributor guidelines for any special notes.
In general, the process looks like this:

1. Fork the project repo

2. Solve/code the problem

3. Submit a Pull Request

4. Wait for feedback

Let's examine each step in some detail. We'll use GitHub for our examples; most online repositories will operate in a similar manner.

Forking the Project Repo

Here, you will create your own local copy of the project repo to do your work on.

Be sure to read any special instructions in the project README on how to get the project up and running.

In GitHub, you can simply use the "Fork" button to start this. You can find it in the upper right part of your screen:

You will be prompted for a name in your own account for your fork of the repo:

Create a new fork

A *fork* is a copy of a repository. Forking a repository allows you to freely experiment with changes without affecting the original project. View existing forks.

Owner *   Repository name *

Kiresorg / sbuttons

By default, forks are named the same as their parent repository. You can customize the name to distinguish it further.

Description (optional)

:bulb: Simple buttons you can use easily for your next project.

Create fork

Solving/Coding the Issue

As you're solving the issue, keep a few things in mind:

- Pay attention to any coding style guidelines provided for the project.

- Make sure the project will run as expected, and that any provided tests pass.

- Comment your code as needed to help future devs.

Submitting a Pull Request

Now that you've got a solution for the issue, you will ask the project maintainers to review it and (hopefully) merge it into their repo. You can start PR creation in GitHub right from the original repo.

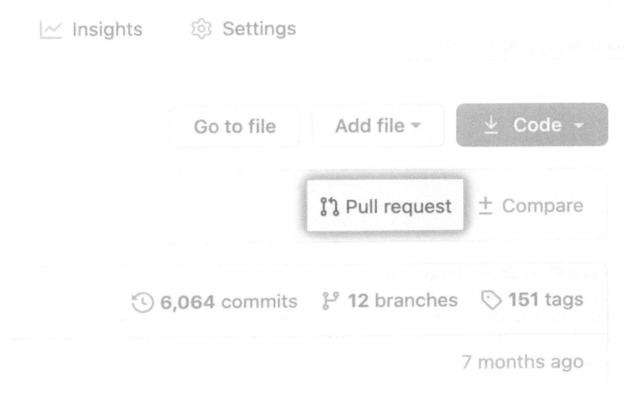

Setting up the branch comparison

This brings up a "compare" page. Be sure to select "compare across forks".

Choosing the branches to merge

Important: pay close attention to which branches you want to merge.

First, select the desired branch in the original repo. Typically this will be the main branch, but be sure to check the contributor guidelines here.

The branch in your forked repo

Next, select the feature branch from your forked repo – the one where you did your work:

Give your PR a title and description

Best practice here: Don't be overly wordy. You can explain your approach, but you should let your code/comments speak for themselves. Maintainers are often tight on time; make your PR easy to read and review.

Create the Pull Request

After a review, click "Create Pull Request". You've done it – your first PR for an open source project is submitted!

Waiting for Feedback

You are likely anxious to hear back on your PR. Please check contributor guidelines for what to expect here – often it will be a while until you hear back, and maintainers may not want you to nudge them.

If there are any points to address in your PR, you will be notified – in GitHub, the whole conversation will be attached to the PR. Watch your email for notifications.

Try to respond quickly to comments on your PR. Maintainers appreciate this.

If you need to refactor your code, do so and then commit the changes. You will likely not need to notify the maintainer; the SCM platform will notify them of the commit, so they can look at the PR again – but again, check the contributor guidelines on this point.

SUMMARY

Getting started in contributing to open source can appear daunting – but don't hesitate. The culture in the FOSS community is typically inviting and inclusive. If you're strategic about how you get started, before long you will have a good record of contributions. Along the way, you will become a better engineer, have a chance to make the projects you love even better, and form relationships that can last throughout your career.

FURTHER READING
Available for Purchase on Amazon

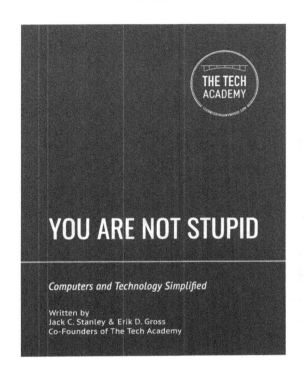

FURTHER READING
Available for Purchase on Amazon

FURTHER READING
Available for Purchase on Amazon

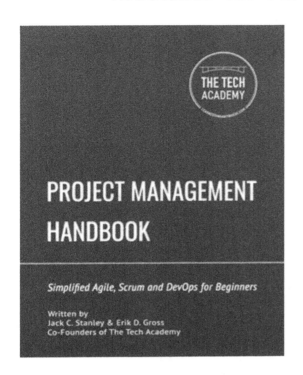

FURTHER READING
Available for Purchase on Amazon

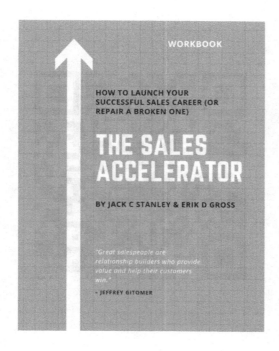

FURTHER READING
Available for Purchase on Amazon

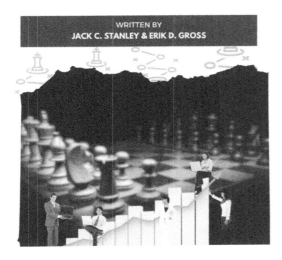

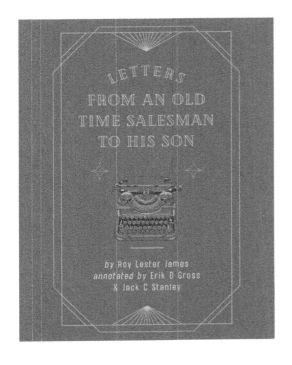

Made in the USA
Monee, IL
12 April 2024

56535881R00031